Written by Alfonso Hanim

BEGINNER'S GUIDE TO NFTS

Co

Table of Contents

Introduction

Non-fungible tokens (NFT) are a relatively new concept that is changing the way that we think about digital assets. Non-fungible tokens are collectible unique tokens that can be owned by a single individual.

The first NFTs were released by CryptoKitties, a blockchain-based game where players can collect, buy, and sell digital cats. The game was so popular that it crashed the Ethereum network.

Since then, developers have created a variety of NFT games that are similar to CryptoKitties. These games are called crypto collectibles.

Crypto collectibles are similar to traditional collectibles in many ways. They're both unique, scarce, and fungible. But they're also different. Traditional collectibles like baseball cards or Beanie Babies are owned by a single individual. Crypto collectibles, on the other hand, are owned by multiple individuals.

Since its inception, the crypto collectibles market has grown rapidly, and today, Crypto art, CryptoPunks, and Crypto Kitties are among the most popular crypto collectibles.

This book is for the beginner who is interested in collecting and trading collectibles. It will help you understand the basics of crypto collectibles and how to trade them. People who are also interested in blockchain technology and want to learn more NFTs will find this book useful.
You will start by learning about the non-fungible token (NFT) and the types of NFTs. After that, you'll learn how to buy collectibles and how to trade them. You will also learn how to use the Crypto Collectibles website.

By the end of this book, you will know all the basics of the Crypto Collectibles market.

Chapter 1: Non-Fungible Tokens

What does Non-Fungible mean?

Non-Fungibility is the property of a good or a commodity whose individual units are considered unique. A Non-Fungible Token (NFT) is a crypto token that has this property.

In other words, if we think of it in terms of the real world, it is like having a share in an asset like gold or silver. The shares are not fungible and are all unique because they represent the asset. So if I own 1% of an ounce of gold, then I own 1% of that particular gold bar. However, I cannot trade my 1% for someone else's 1% of the same gold bar.

The main point here is that NFTs are completely unique and cannot be replicated.

Why do we need Non-Fungible Tokens?

Imagine a situation where you have a non-fungible token representing a car, let's say an Aston Martin DB9. You have spent time and money collecting this token and have used it to pay for a service. However, the owner of the Aston Martin has used the same token to buy some parts for his car. What happens if you decide to sell your token? It is no longer valid because it has been used for two different things, and this means that you will not get the value that you would have gotten if it was still valid.

This is one of the issues that can be solved by using NFTs because they are completely unique and cannot be replicated. So once they are sold or transferred, they cannot be used again by anyone else on any other platform because each individual unit is unique. The owner can use it in any way he wants as long as he owns it; but if he transfers it to someone else, then he loses all rights to it.

Non-fungible tokens are unique digital assets. They are not divisible and have unique properties that make them a valuable digital asset.

The purpose of a fungible token is to be interchangeable with other tokens. They serve as a currency that can be transferred from one individual to another.

A non-fungible token (NFT) is a token where every single unit is unique. It is not interchangeable. The unit can be unique based on the combination of its properties such as its name, image, and information about the owner. It can also be unique based on its value.

A good representation is a collectible card. For example, if I have a card of Michael Jordan and you have a card of Michael Jordan, there is no way to exchange our cards. The details of the card, such as the number, the image, and the name of the player, are unique.

The unit is also unique because it has a specific value. Collectible cards have an assigned value. The most expensive card of Michael Jordan has an assigned value that is higher than a common card of Michael Jordan.

NFTs can also be unique because they represent an asset. They can represent ownership of a land, a building, a car, or any other physical and digital asset. If you have an asset, you can give it a unique identifier. You can give it a unique identifier by linking it to a blockchain.

It is possible to build a digital asset registry and use the blockchain as the registry to store all the assets. This can be done using NFTs.The attributes of a NFT can be used to make it unique. The combination of these attributes makes the NFT unique.

It is also possible to use the blockchain to create a unique identifier that links the physical assets to a blockchain. By linking the physical assets to a blockchain, it is possible to create digital representations of these assets. This makes it possible to use NFTs to represent these assets.

Using NFTs to represent physical assets makes it possible for individuals and businesses to use blockchain technology. If you want to buy a house, you can store the information about the house in a digital asset registry and use NFTs as unique identifiers for that house.

This way, if you want to sell the house, you can transfer ownership of that specific NFT to another individual. The individual will receive ownership of that specific NFT and will have full control over that NFT. They can transfer it again or sell it on an exchange.

What is a Fungible Token?

Fungibility is the property of a good or a commodity whose individual units are interchangeable. It is also known as "fungible goods" or "fungible assets". For example, if I own a gold bar, then I can trade it for another gold bar of the same size and weight without any problem.

A fungible token is any token that has this property. If we take the same example as above where we have an Aston Martin DB9 token and someone else has used it to buy some parts for his car, then this would not be a problem because it is fungible. If I decide to sell my token, then anyone can use it to buy parts for their car because they are all the same and they all represent the same Aston Martin DB9.

Non-Fungible Tokens vs Fungible Tokens

The difference between non-fungible tokens and fungible tokens is the way in which they are used and transferred from one person to another. A fungible token can be transferred from one person to another, and it does not matter who owns it; but with a non-fungible token, once it has been transferred to someone else, then it is no longer valid and cannot be used by anyone else.

A good example of a fungible token is Ether (ETH) which is the native token for the Ethereum blockchain. You can buy and sell ETH as you want, and there is no problem with that because it is completely interchangeable. However, once you have bought ETH from someone else, then you do not have any control over what happens to it because it can be used in any way that the new owner wants to use it.

NFTs are different because they are completely unique and cannot be replicated or copied like other digital assets. So if you own an NFT, then you own all rights to it until you decide to transfer or trade it with someone else.

How is this different from the use of fungible tokens?

When you buy a fungible token, you buy it with the intention of using it as a currency.

For example, if you buy a Bitcoin, you can use it to pay for goods and services. If you have 1 BTC, it does not matter if that BTC is from the same wallet or from another wallet. You can still use it to pay for goods and services.

If you own an NFT, such as a card of Michael Jordan, you do not want to sell it to another individual because the individual will not be able to use that specific NFT. It will be useless for them because they do not own the card. They will only own a unique identifier that represents ownership of that specific card.

A lot of developers are using non-fungible tokens in their applications because they represent digital assets and physical assets. This makes them valuable digital assets that are used by businesses and individuals on a daily basis. They are being used in games such as CryptoKitties and Rarebits. It is also possible to create smart contracts with non-fungible tokens such as land registry records or event tickets. The blockchain technology is being used by governments to store information about assets.

How different is it from ERC20?

The ERC20 token standard was created to create fungible tokens. This means that every single token is identical to another token. The properties of the tokens are identical and the value of the tokens is identical.

The properties of the ERC20 tokens are only visible on the blockchain. The Ethereum blockchain can be used to check how many tokens exist and how much they are worth.

With NFTs, it is possible to create unique identifiers that represent ownership of a digital asset or a physical asset. These identifiers can be stored on a blockchain. The blockchain will store information about these unique identifiers and it will be possible to check them on a public ledger.

This makes it possible for individuals and businesses to use NFTs in their applications because they can transfer ownership of these assets from one individual to another without using intermediaries such as banks or other third parties. This reduces costs and makes it easier for individuals and businesses to trade digital assets or physical assets such as real estate, artwork, jewellery, cars, or any other physical asset that can be digitized using blockchain
technology.

How is this different from Ethereum?

The Ethereum blockchain supports smart contracts where fungible tokens are used as payment for services or goods.

If you have an ERC20 token, you can use it to pay for goods and services on the Ethereum blockchain.

The Ethereum blockchain also supports ERC721 which is a standard for non-fungible tokens.

Ethereum is the first blockchain that supports smart contracts where fungible tokens are used as payment for services or goods. The Ethereum blockchain is also the first blockchain that supports smart contracts where non-fungible tokens are used as unique identifiers that represent ownership of digital assets or physical assets.

This means that Ethereum is the first blockchain that supports smart contracts where fungible tokens are used as payment for services or goods and where non-fungible tokens are used as unique identifiers that represent ownership of digital assets or physical assets.

The Fungibility Problem

This brings us to one of the main problems with cryptocurrencies – fungibility. This means that if you own 10 Bitcoins (BTC), then anyone can take those 10 BTC from you and trade them with someone else for whatever they want without you being able to do anything about it. This makes Bitcoin less desirable because you cannot control what happens to your coins once they are transferred or traded with someone else.

Fungibility is a problem that can be solved by using NFTs. In fact, one of the biggest use cases for NFTs is in the digital asset space. This is because digital assets are already unique and can be used in any way that you want to as long as you own them. So if you buy a digital asset, then you have complete control over it until you decide to transfer it to someone else.

One of the main benefits of using NFTs for digital assets is that they can be sold or traded on different platforms without any problem because they are completely unique and cannot be replicated. They also solve the problem of double spending since each individual unit cannot be used more than once. This means that they cannot be copied or cloned like other digital assets like ERC-20 tokens.

Chapter 2: The Technicalities of NFTs

What is Ethereum?

Ethereum was created by Vitalik Buterin in 2013. It is a blockchain-based decentralized platform that runs smart contracts.

Smart contracts are essentially computer programs that automatically execute the terms of an agreement between two or more parties.

Ethereum smart contracts can be used to facilitate, verify, and enforce the negotiation or performance of virtually any type of contract.

These types of smart contracts are self-executing, as they are programmed with specific instructions that cannot be altered once the contract is established. They run on a decentralized virtual machine called Ethereum Virtual Machine (EVM). The EVM operates independently of any specific blockchain platform and even its own network, as it is designed to operate in conjunction with any blockchain platform that supports smart contracts. The EVM allows smart contracts to use an unlimited amount of computing power and memory capacity for their operation. As a result, Ethereum's decentralized apps can operate autonomously without having to pay for external resources such as servers or databases.

The EVM also uses gas to run its operations; users must pay for this gas with Ether (ETH), which is Ethereum's native cryptocurrency token. Every time a user sends data or money in a transaction on the Ethereum network, they must pay for the gas that is required to process the transaction. This incentivizes miners to include the transaction in the blockchain, as they are compensated with ETH for doing so.

It is important to note that there are two types of accounts on Ethereum: external accounts and contract accounts. External accounts are controlled by private keys, and these keys are usually stored on users' computers or smartphones. Contract accounts, on the other hand, can only be controlled by their corresponding private keys. Contract accounts do not have any public key or address associated with them, as they can only be accessed through their corresponding private key.

How does Ethereum work?

Ethereum's native cryptocurrency token is called Ether (ETH). ETH is used to pay for gas, which is the internal pricing for running operations on the Ethereum network.

Whenever a user wants to run an operation on the Ethereum network, they must send a transaction request to the network. The transaction request contains all of the data needed to execute the operation, as well as information about how much ETH they are willing to pay for it. If there are enough unspent transaction outputs (UTXOs) available in their account, then they will have enough ETH to pay for the gas required by their operation. However, if there are not enough UTXOs available in their account, then they will need to use some of their ETH balance or credit some ETH from another account in order to pay for the gas required by their operation.

The process of sending a transaction request and paying for its gas is referred to as "mining" on Ethereum. This process is similar to mining Bitcoin; miners send out a block containing all of the data needed by a transaction and include a small fee with it in order to be compensated for their services. Miners who successfully add this block into the blockchain receive the transaction fee as a reward.

The execution of an operation is known as "gas" on Ethereum. Every operation has a gas limit and a gas price, which are used to determine how much ETH will be required to pay for the gas needed by the operation. Gas is essentially a measure of computational effort; the more complicated an operation is, the more gas it will require. The amount of ETH required to pay for this gas depends on its price, which is determined by the user when they send their transaction request. If the user sets a high price for their transaction, then they will have to pay more ETH for its gas; if they set a low price, then they will have to pay less ETH for its gas.

Every operation has an associated amount of "gas" that must be paid in order to execute it successfully. This amount is also known as "gas limit" or "gas limit per block" (depending on whether or not it is set per block or per transaction). If this amount of gas is not provided with the transaction request, then the network will reject it and refuse to execute it. In addition, if this amount of gas exceeds that which can be paid for with the user's ETH balance, then the network will also reject it and refuse to execute it.

It is important to note that the gas limit is not necessarily equal to the amount of gas required by an operation. For example, an operation that requires only a small amount of gas might have a high gas limit in order to compensate for future changes in the price of ETH. In addition, an operation might require more than one block to be executed successfully; in this case, each block will have its own gas limit.

The "gas price" is determined by the user when they send their transaction request. This price is used to determine how much ETH they will need to pay for their transaction's gas. The higher the price set by the user, the more ETH they will need to pay for their transaction's gas; if they set a low price, then they will only need to pay a small amount of ETH for their transaction's gas. The total amount of ETH required by a transaction depends on both its "gas limit" and its "gas price"; it can be calculated using this formula:

Gas Price * Gas Limit = Amount of ETH Required

The "gas limit" is determined by the amount of gas required by an operation. This amount can be calculated using this formula:

Gas Limit = Gas Required / Gas Price

What is ERC-20 and ERC-721?

ERC-20 and ERC-721 are two different types of smart contracts that can be used to create NFTs.

ERC-20 is a technical standard that defines a set of rules for creating tokens on the Ethereum blockchain. Tokens created using this standard can be stored in any Ethereum wallet that supports ERC-20 tokens.

ERC-721 is an improvement over ERC-20, as it defines a set of rules for creating non-fungible tokens (NFTs) on the Ethereum blockchain. NFTs are unique digital assets that are not divisible or interchangeable with one another; they can only be transferred in their entirety from one owner to another. Each NFT also has its own unique identifier, which makes it easier to track and verify its ownership history and provenance. Tokens created using this standard can only be stored in wallets that support ERC-721 tokens. The most popular wallet for storing ERC-721 tokens is CryptoKitties' own proprietary KittyWallet app, which has been downloaded more than 250,000 times since its launch in December 2017. CryptoKitties itself was the first ever blockchain game to launch an NFT marketplace for users to buy, sell, and breed their digital cats.

What are the requirements for an NFT to be ERC-721 compliant?

An NFT must meet the following requirements in order to be considered ERC-721 compliant:

It must be owned by a single address. This means that you cannot have multiple owners of an NFT, just like you cannot have multiple owners of a car or house.

It must not have any fungible copies. If there are multiple copies of an NFT then it is not unique and thus not non-fungible. This means that you cannot have one copy of a token and another copy of that same token with the same balance on two different addresses.

You must have a fixed supply (i.e., there can only ever be one "first edition" CryptoKitty). It must be possible to transfer ownership (i.e., if I give you my NFT then it now belongs to you). It must be impossible to modify ownership information (i.e., I can't make it look like I'm still the owner of the NFT even though I gave it to you).

ERC-721 is very specific about what properties an NFT must have in order to be considered ERC-721 compliant.

What are some examples of ERC-721 compliant NFTs?

There are a lot of different types of ERC-721 compliant NFTs. They include: CryptoKitties, CryptoPunks, Decentraland, Cryptobots, Axie Infinity, Gods Unchained and many more.

You can buy ERC-721 compliant NFTs on websites like OpenSea and RareBits. These websites act as a marketplace for buying and selling non-fungible tokens.

How are NFTs created?

NFTs can be created using a special smart contract called an "ERC-721 smart contract". ERC-721 smart contracts are designed to be used with Ethereum, and they can only be accessed by their owner or owners. They are similar to normal Ethereum smart contracts in that they have a unique address and can only be accessed by their owner or owners; however, they are different from normal Ethereum smart contracts in that they do not have any gas limit or gas price associated with them. In addition, the information stored on an ERC-721 smart contract cannot be changed once it is stored on the blockchain; any changes made to it will result in its permanent destruction. As a result, ERC-721 smart contracts cannot be used for transactions or data storage; they can only be used for creating NFTs.

Once an ERC-721 smart contract has been created, it can then issue new tokens at any time to its owner or owners. This process is known as "minting" on Ethereum; tokens are minted when new assets are added to the blockchain by creating a new smart contract.

How are NFTs stored?

ERC-721 smart contracts are stored on the Ethereum blockchain, and as a result, NFTs can be stored in any Ethereum wallet that supports ERC-721 tokens. Some of the most popular wallets for storing ERC-721 tokens include:

MetaMask: This browser extension is available for both Chrome and Firefox. It can be used to interact with websites that support Ethereum by creating and signing transactions on the blockchain. It also allows users to access their Ethereum wallet, which can be used to store ERC-721 tokens. MetaMask currently has more than 500,000 active users worldwide.

Coinbase Wallet: This wallet is available on both iOS and Android platforms, and it can be used to store any cryptocurrency that is supported by Coinbase, including Ether (ETH), Bitcoin (BTC), Litecoin (LTC), and more than 90 other coins and tokens. It also supports Ethereum's ERC-20 standard, which means it can be used to store ERC-20 tokens like CryptoKitties' own proprietary KittyWallet app. As of January 2019, Coinbase Wallet has been downloaded more than 100,000 times.

MyEtherWallet: This is a popular open-source wallet that can be used to store ERC-20 tokens, as well as other types of tokens that are supported by Ethereum. It can be used to store any ERC-20 token that is created using the Ethereum blockchain.

MyCrypto: This is another open-source wallet that can be used to store Ether (ETH), ERC-20 tokens, and other types of tokens that are supported by Ethereum. It is also compatible with ERC-721 smart contracts, which means it can be used to store NFTs.

MetaMask, Coinbase Wallet, MyEtherWallet, and MyCrypto are all compatible with CryptoKitties' KittyWallet app. They are also compatible with any other ERC-721 smart contract or application that supports NFTs and can issue new NFTs at any time to its owner or owners. CryptoKitties itself was the first ever blockchain game to launch an NFT marketplace for users to buy, sell, and breed their digital cats; it has since been followed by several other blockchain games such as CryptoAlpaca, CryptoFighters, and EtherTanks.

What is the difference between NFTs and other types of tokens?

NFTs are similar to other types of tokens in that they can be created on the Ethereum blockchain; however, they are different from other types of tokens in that they cannot be divided or exchanged for one another. As a result, they have unique identifiers that make it easier to track and verify their ownership history and provenance. NFTs are also unique in that their owners can choose to have them destroyed if they want to permanently remove them from the blockchain. This process is known as "destruction" on Ethereum; NFTs can be destroyed by calling the "burn()" function within an ERC-721 smart contract. Once an NFT has been destroyed, it cannot be recovered or transferred to another owner; it can only be stored on the blockchain forever. The only way to permanently remove an NFT from the blockchain is by destroying it, as this prevents anyone else from accessing it or stealing it.

There are two main types of NFTs: Crypto Collectibles and Crypto Assets.

Crypto Collectibles:
These are non-fungible tokens that act as unique assets, similar to how the physical world has collectibles like baseball cards, comics, etc. The most famous example of a crypto collectible is CryptoKitties.

Cryptoassets:

These are non-fungible tokens that act as shares in an underlying business or project. The most famous example of a crypto asset is Ethereum. There are many other crypto assets such as Bitcoin, ZCash, Augur, Golem, etc. which you can buy on exchanges like Coinbase Pro and Finance or through a wallet like Metamask.

The most important distinction between crypto collectibles and crypto assets is that the latter can be traded for money while the former cannot. This is due to the fact that crypto collectibles are purely for collecting and cannot be exchanged for value.

What is the underlying technology behind NFTs?

NFTs are based on the Ethereum blockchain and use smart contracts to determine ownership. The term "smart contract" is used a lot in the crypto space, but what does it actually mean? A smart contract is essentially an immutable, digital contract that can be programmed to execute certain actions if a specific set of conditions are met. It is a piece of code that automatically executes itself when specific events occur.

The main purpose of a smart contract is to act as an escrow between two parties. It allows for more efficient and secure transactions between two parties because it eliminates the need for an intermediary or middleman. For example, if you want to buy a house from someone but don't have enough money at the time, you can enter into a smart contract with them so that they hold onto your money until you get the funds necessary to pay them back. You both agree on the terms of this smart contract and then your money will be held in escrow until you come up with the funds to pay them back.

This brings us back to NFTs. How do they work with smart contracts? NFTs allow for digital assets like video game characters or collectibles to be tokenized on the blockchain. This means that they can be used in smart contracts. For example, let's say you are a video game developer and you want to allow users to buy digital characters with their money. You can use NFTs to tokenize these characters and program them into a smart contract so that users can purchase them with their Ethereum (or other) tokens. This is how CryptoKitties work.

To summarize, NFTs are digital assets that are used in smart contracts for things like digital collectibles or game items.

Chapter 3: History of NFTs

Crypto is all about decentralization. It is a type of technology that is slowly making its way into our daily lives. And what is decentralized technology? Well, the answer to that question can be quite complex. But, we can take a look at it as something that has no central authority or governing body. In other words, it's a type of technology that is owned by the people and not a company or organization.

With this in mind, we can easily see how the concept of NFTs makes sense within the realm of crypto. If you're new to the crypto space, you may have no idea what NFTs are.

Let's take a look at the history of NFTs and how they came to be.

The Bitcoin Boom (and Crash… and Boom):

It's been a long road for crypto, but it all started with Bitcoin. As the story goes, Satoshi Nakamoto came up with the idea of a decentralized currency that was not controlled by any one central authority.

With this in mind, Satoshi created the first ever cryptocurrency in 2009. In order to verify transactions on the blockchain, miners would need to solve complex mathematical equations. This process is known as mining and is what led to Bitcoin's rise in popularity.

At first, Bitcoin was pretty worthless and not many people were interested in it. However, over time it became more valuable and more people began to use it as a way to send money around the world without having to pay outrageous fees from banks or other financial institutions.

This led to the rise of Bitcoin and all other cryptocurrencies. As the popularity of Bitcoin grew, so did the value of each coin. It reached a peak in December 2017 when it was valued at $19,000 per coin. This caused a massive influx of people into the crypto space.

As you can imagine, this led to quite a bit of confusion for many people who were new to crypto. They were wondering how they could invest in this "amazing" technology that was supposed to be decentralized and give everyone more control over their money. So, many people bought into what is known as "pump and dump" schemes where they would buy low and sell high – like in any other stock market or market in general.

But this wasn't always the case with crypto investors…at first. When Bitcoin first came out, it was intended for investors who understood how blockchain technology worked and what it meant for the future of cryptocurrency as a whole. But then it exploded in popularity when "crypto bros" started pumping up the price with their ridiculous amounts of money.

This caused an influx of new investors into the crypto space who had no idea what they were doing. This led to the crash of 2018, which saw the price of Bitcoin drop from $19,000 per coin to around $3,200.

Where and when did NFTs first appear?

We've talked about how Bitcoin led to the rise of cryptocurrency. But, there was another piece of technology that came before Bitcoin and paved the way for it to exist.

It's called a blockchain. The blockchain is what allows cryptocurrency to exist. Without a blockchain, you wouldn't be able to send or receive money on the internet.

Now, we know that NFTs have become very popular in recent years and they're going to be a big part of the future of crypto.

But, where did they come from? Well, it all started with an idea that was thought up by a man named Nick Szabo.

Nick Szabo is an American computer scientist and cryptographer who has been credited with the creation of the first ever smart contract. This contract was based on a game called "The Fermi Paradox" which he designed back in 1995.

In this game, users would send a digital asset to another user without using any third-party services like banks or PayPal. In order to do this, you would need to send the digital asset to an anonymous public key address – and then hope that it made its way to the intended recipient. If it didn't make its way there, then you would have lost your money forever – unless someone else sent it to them for you.

The NFTs of Today:

With this in mind, we can see how Nick Szabo came up with the idea for NFTs long before crypto was even around. Nowadays, there are many different types of NFTs being used in various industries and projects throughout the world. The biggest names in NFTs include CryptoKitties, Etheremon, and CryptoPunks.

These are just a few of the projects that have made their mark on the world of NFTs. There are many more out there that you can find on sites like Enjin. Enjin is a platform that is built specifically for creating and trading NFTs. It's like an online store where you can buy and sell various digital assets.

Now, it's important to note that these digital assets are not real-world items – they're based on blockchain technology and therefore cannot be touched or seen by the naked eye. However, there are some NFTs that have physical representations as well – such as CryptoPunks or GigaPets from Rare Bits.

We've also mentioned CryptoKitties which is one of the most popular NFTs out there right now. These Kitties are digital pets based on blockchain technology that people can buy, sell, breed, or even exchange with one another for ETH (Ethereum). These

Kitties come in different breeds with different attributes – such as fur color or how many eggs they produce per breeding cycle. Some of these cats have become extremely valuable – like the Kitty that sold for $140,000.

Etheremon is another popular NFT project that uses blockchain technology to create digital monsters based on the Ethereum blockchain. These monsters can be used in battle and are completely unique – so there is no way to get them again once they're sold or traded.

The popularity of NFTs is growing every day and it seems like they're here to stay. Many companies are getting into the space by launching their own NFT projects. But, it's important to remember that these projects can be very confusing and risky for investors who don't understand how blockchain technology works.

CryptoKitties

CryptoKitties is a blockchain-based game that lets you buy, sell, and breed virtual cats. It was created by Axiom Zen, a Canadian company based in Vancouver. The game became popular with the release of CryptoKitties in November 2017.

CryptoKitties is a prime example of how NFTs can be used to create decentralized applications (DApps). It is one of the first games to use blockchain technology and is the best example of how it can be used to create something fun and enjoyable for the public.

The main goal of CryptoKitties is to breed rare cats that are valuable on the marketplace. You start out with two cats that you can then breed together and hope for rare offspring.

There are many things that make CryptoKitties a great game. The most important of these is the fact that it's fun to play. It's an interactive game that lets you create new virtual cats with unique features and attributes. This makes it more than just a game. It is a tool for creative expression, as well as an investment opportunity.

If you're new to the crypto space, you may be wondering how exactly CryptoKitties work.

How Does CryptoKitties Work?

CryptoKitties works through the use of smart contracts on the Ethereum blockchain. This means that the Kitties are owned by their owners and not by anyone else. You can buy, sell, or breed your kitties on the marketplace and no one can stop you from doing so. All transactions are recorded on the blockchain and there is no central authority in charge of them.

In addition to this, each Kitty has its own set of unique characteristics or traits. These traits include color, pattern, eyes color, and coat pattern – all which are randomly generated when a new Kitty is created on the blockchain platform. These traits can be passed down from parent to child during breeding sessions which results in new traits and new combinations.

All of these traits and their values are recorded on the blockchain. This means that they cannot be tampered with or changed in any way. And because the kitties are owned by their owners, there is no central authority that can decide to take them away from you.

How Do You Buy CryptoKitties?

The first thing you need to do if you want to buy a CryptoKitty is to create an account on the platform. Once you've done this, you can then visit the marketplace and purchase a Kitty from one of the sellers there. You will then be given a private key that you can use to access your Kitty on the blockchain.

This private key is unique to your account and only works with your specific Kitty. So, if someone else has access to it, they won't be able to access your Kitty – even if they have an identical one of their own! This means that there is no way for anyone else but you to get hold of your kitty without your permission.

How Do You Breed CryptoKitties?

In order for two Kitties to breed together, they must both have a unique genetic code. The Kitties can be owned by different people and come from different backgrounds. However, they must both have the same number of attributes or genes in order to breed together.

Once you've found two Kitties that you want to breed together, you can visit the breeding page on the CryptoKitties website. This page will give you all of the information that you need in order to know whether or not your Kitties are compatible.

If they are compatible, you can then choose a date and time for your breeding session to take place. After this, it's up to the blockchain platform to determine whether or not your Kitties have a new offspring that is born during this time period. If they do, then you will be notified via email and your Kitty will receive a new set of traits from its parents!

How Much Are CryptoKitties Worth?

When CryptoKitties first launched, their price was relatively low compared to how much they are worth today. At first, they were only worth around $10 each which made them accessible for just about anyone who wanted one! And with more and more people getting involved with CryptoKitties each day, their value has increased considerably.

Today, a single CryptoKitty can be worth anywhere between $100 and $20,000. And with more people becoming interested in them each day, their value is only going to increase in the future. So, if you're thinking about getting involved with CryptoKitties, now is the perfect time to do so!

Are CryptoKitties Legal?

Yes, it is completely legal to own a CryptoKitty and they are completely legal on the blockchain platform that they run on. They have been deemed as an investment asset by the United States Securities and Exchange Commission (SEC) which means that you must be at least 18 years old in order to purchase one. This means that it is also illegal for anyone under 18 years old to buy a CryptoKitty! In addition to this, it is illegal for anyone who does not have access to their own private key (and the associated Kitty) to purchase one of these Kitties. So if you're thinking about buying a Kitty for someone else as a gift, make sure that they are at least 18 years old before doing so!

Crypto Art

Crypto is all about decentralization. It is a type of technology that is slowly making its way into our daily lives. And what is decentralized technology? Well, the answer to that question can be quite complex. But, we can take a look at it as something that has no central authority or governing body. In other words, it's a type of technology that is owned by the people and not a company or organization.

With this in mind, we can easily see how the concept of NFTs makes sense within the realm of crypto. If you're new to the crypto space, you may have no idea what NFTs are.

What is Crypto art?

In short, Crypto Art is the intersection of the blockchain space and the art world. In a more technical sense, it's a form of digital asset that is unique and can be bought and sold on various crypto exchanges.

The first example of crypto art is CryptoKitties. These digital cats can be bought and sold, and they are limited in number. However, there are no specific parameters that govern the creation of these kitties. Each one is unique and can be owned by an individual or a group of people.

These digital assets are similar to stocks in that they have ownership and value, but they're also unique in that there is no set algorithm that determines how many there will be or how they will be created. There are no centralized rules, regulations, or governing bodies governing the creation of these kitties.

Today, digital artists from all around the world are creating unique crypto art. In the future, this will be one of the most exciting industries in the blockchain space. There are many platforms such as OpenSea and RareBits that allow you to buy and sell digital art.

How do you transact in NFTs?

Crypto art is still in its infancy, but that doesn't mean that there aren't ways to buy and sell it. Many people use decentralized exchanges to buy and sell digital art. These exchanges work similarly to stock exchanges, but they have a much more unique and fluid structure.

Many people also use crypto art as a form of investment. They see it as a way to make money, but they also see it as an opportunity to support artists around the world. These artists are creating beautiful works of art that are being bought and sold every day. Some pieces of crypto art have even sold for millions of dollars! It's an exciting time for crypto art, and we can only expect more from this exciting industry in the future.

These are the most popular Crypto art marketplaces:

1. OpenSea

OpenSea is a decentralized marketplace for blockchain-based assets. It's the first marketplace that was created for crypto art.
The company was founded in 2017 by an experienced team of blockchain developers and entrepreneurs. The company is based in San Francisco, California and is a part of the Boost VC accelerator program.

2. RareBits

RareBits is a decentralized exchange for buying and selling digital art and collectibles. The company has been around since 2015, and it's based in Vancouver, Canada. It's also a part of the Boost VC accelerator program.

The company has attracted over 100 different sellers from all around the world to sell their digital art on its platform. Some of these artists have sold their works for over $1 million! In addition to this, there are over 1,000 different assets on the platform from artists all around the world!

3. RarePepe

RarePepe is a decentralized exchange for buying and selling rare Pepe memes. It's one of the most popular and exciting exchanges in the crypto space. It was founded in 2017 by Joe Looney, who was a member of the first graduating class of Boost VC. The company is based in San Francisco, California.

Crypto art is one of the most exciting developments in the blockchain space. We're still very early on in this industry, but it's only going to get bigger and better as time goes on. In fact, we can expect many more companies to create platforms that will allow you to buy and sell digital art online. It's an exciting time for the blockchain space.

We will get into the hype and the boom of Crypto Art in chapter 7.

Chapter 4:
The Economics of NFTs

This chapter will explore the economic considerations of non-fungible tokens (NFTs).

Non-fungible tokens have been a major trend in blockchain gaming, and are still in their infancy. This chapter will lay out the basic ideas behind the economics of NFTs, with an emphasis on collectibles and non-games.

In particular, this chapter will explore the factors that influence the demand for NFTs. It will also explain how NFTs differ from traditional fungible tokens (such as bitcoin and ether) in terms of their economics.

As you read this chapter, you may notice a few similarities between NFTs and collectibles such as baseball cards or trading cards. For example, the value of a non-fungible token may be influenced by factors such as scarcity, provenance, and condition. As we'll see later in this chapter, these are common economic factors that drive the demand for collectibles.

Who are the stakeholders of NFTs

1. Developers

The developer is the person or company that creates the game and owns the code. They are in charge of deploying the game to the blockchain, maintaining it, and adding new features to it.

The developer can be a centralized entity, such as a game studio or blockchain company. Or they can be a decentralized team, such as an open-source community of contributors. In most cases, NFTs will be launched by developers on top of an existing blockchain protocol (such as Ethereum). The developer then creates a smart contract to support their game. The rules of this smart contract determine how the NFTs are minted and transferred between players in the game. The developer also determines what happens when NFTs are destroyed or abandoned (more on this later).

2. Players

The player is any person who plays a game using NFTs and owns them at some point during gameplay. There are many different types of players in any given NFT-based game: first-time users who want to learn how to play; casual players who enjoy regular gameplay; and expert players who participate in high-stakes tournaments with prizes like cars or houses. A player may play just for fun, but they may also play for financial gain.

3. Collectors

The collector is any person who owns NFTs for investment purposes. The most common type of collector is an NFT investor, or someone who purchases NFTs in order to sell them at a higher price in the future. There are many other types of collectors as well, including speculators and NFT traders. Collectors are interested in any game that uses NFTs, regardless of how popular it is. Some collectors are highly selective about which games they support, while others collect as many different types of games as possible.

4. Traders

The trader is a player who specializes in buying and selling NFTs to make a profit. They can be players or collectors, but their primary goal is to buy low and sell high rather than to play the game itself. Most traders are active on secondary markets such as centralized exchanges or decentralized exchanges (DEXes). A DEX is an online market where buyers and sellers can trade with each other directly without the use of a middleman (like an exchange). There are several ways that traders make money from NFTs: they can sell them at higher prices than they paid; they can short sell them; or they can trade them on margin.

5. Speculators

The speculator is a player who buys NFTs in order to sell them at a higher price in the future. They may buy NFTs from other players or from the developer, depending on their strategy. For example, they may purchase an NFT at a discount during its presale period and then sell it for more once it becomes more popular. Or they may purchase an NFT that is highly sought after by collectors and hold onto it until it appreciates in value.

6. Investors

The investor is a player who purchases NFTs as part of a portfolio of assets (or with borrowed money). They expect to make a profit on their investment over time through price appreciation or dividends (more on this later). The most common type of investor is an asset manager, or someone who manages other people's money and uses investment strategies such as value investing, growth investing, or momentum investing. Investors can also be hedge funds, family offices, angel investors, venture capitalists, and others. They are interested in any game that uses NFTs regardless of how popular it is. However, most of them are more selective about which games they support than collectors are.

7. NFT Marketplace

The NFT marketplace is any marketplace where NFTs are bought and sold. This can be a centralized exchange, a decentralized exchange, or a specialized trading platform for NFTs. The NFT marketplace can also be the game itself, if the game supports in-game trading of NFTs.

NFT Economics: The Factors that Influence Demand

The demand for an NFT is determined by many different factors, including scarcity, provenance, condition, desirability, utility, liquidity, and speculation. Some of these factors are unique to non-fungible tokens (NFTs), while others are shared with traditional fungible tokens (such as bitcoin and ether). In this section we'll explore each factor in more detail. We'll start with some basic economic concepts that are relevant to both types of tokens before we dive into how they apply to non-fungible tokens specifically.

Key Economic Concepts: Scarcity & Utility

When it comes to economics, there are two main factors that influence the demand for a good or service: scarcity and utility.

Scarcity refers to the limited availability of a good or service. If a good is scarce, then it's more valuable because there is less of it available. If something is scarce, it's also in demand because people want to get their hands on it before it runs out.

The utility of a good or service refers to its usefulness and how much value people derive from it. The more useful something is, the more people will want to have it in their lives. This may be because they need the thing itself (such as food or water), or because they want to use it as an input for other goods and services (such as a computer for playing games). In either case, people derive utility from something that they can use in their lives. As a result, an item with high utility will tend to have high demand and thus be worth more money.

The key takeaway here is that if something has both scarcity and utility, then people will want to own it at all costs — which leads us into our next topic: non-fungible tokens (NFTs).

Here are the other factors which affects the demand for NFTs:

1. Provenance

Provenance refers to the history of ownership of an NFT. This includes things like: who owned it previously, how it was acquired, where it has been, and what the item was used for.

As you can imagine, provenance is a huge factor in determining the value of an NFT. For example, if someone were to find a rare Pokemon card from 1996 with mint condition and no wear and tear on it, then that card would be worth much more than an average one from the same year. That's because people would want to own this card not only because it's rare but also because they could show off its incredible provenance. In other words, the provenance of an NFT will affect its demand just as much as its scarcity and utility.

The importance of provenance becomes even more apparent when you think about collectibles like art or wine — which are often sold based on their story rather than their utility or scarcity. For example, if someone were to find a rare Picasso painting from 1917 that was never sold at auction before, then they would probably pay millions for it — even though Picasso paintings are relatively common compared to other types of art. That's because the painting's provenance (or story) is what makes it so valuable.

2. Condition

Condition refers to the state of an NFT and how well it has been taken care of. For example, if someone buys a rare baseball card in mint condition, then they can expect to pay more for it than they would for an average one in poor condition. The same applies to art or wine: a painting that has been preserved well over time will have much more value than one that has been damaged by water or age. In other words, the condition of an NFT will affect its demand just as much as its scarcity and utility.

3. Desirability

Desirability refers to how desirable an NFT is in the eyes of people. This includes things like: what use case the item serves, whether or not people want to collect it, and how unique it is compared to other items of its kind. The desirability of an NFT will affect its demand just as much as its scarcity and utility. For example, a rare baseball card from 1996 may be worth millions because people love collecting baseball cards from that year — but it may only be worth a few dollars if no one wants to collect it.

4. Utility

Utility refers to the usefulness of an NFT and how much value people derive from it. For example, if someone buys a rare baseball card from 1996, then they can use it as a collectible — or they can sell it for cash if they want to. In either case, the baseball card will have utility in the eyes of its owner and thus will be worth more money than an average one from the same year. The same applies to art or wine: a painting that has a special use case (such as holding valuable documents) will have much more value than one that doesn't serve any purpose at all. In other words, the utility of an NFT will affect its demand just as much as its scarcity and provenance.

5. Liquidity

Liquidity refers to how easy it is to convert an NFT into cash — or any other asset for that matter. If something is liquid, then you can easily convert it into another asset — such as cash or another cryptocurrency — whenever you want without having to worry about losing value in the process. If something is not liquid, then you may have difficulty converting it into cash or another asset.

For example, if someone were to buy a rare baseball card from 1996, then they would probably have no problem selling it for cash. In other words, the baseball card is liquid because there are plenty of people who want to buy it — and those people are willing to pay top dollar for it. On the other hand, if someone were to buy a rare Picasso painting from 1917, then they would probably have a very hard time selling it for cash — even though the painting is more valuable than the baseball card. That's because Picasso paintings are less liquid than baseball cards because there are fewer people who want to buy them — and those people are only willing to pay top dollar for them in special circumstances.

6. Speculation

Speculation refers to how much value an NFT has in terms of potential future use cases and price appreciation. For example, if someone buys a rare baseball card from 1996 because they think that its value will increase over time due to limited supply and high demand, then they are speculating on its future price appreciation — which means that the NFT has speculative value in their eyes. On the other hand, if someone buys a rare Picasso painting from 1917 because they think that its value will increase over time due to limited supply and high demand, then they are also speculating on its future price appreciation — which means that the NFT has speculative value in their eyes.

In other words, speculation is a factor that affects the demand for NFTs just as much as scarcity, provenance, condition, desirability, utility, and liquidity. In fact, speculation is the only factor in this list that is unique to NFTs — because it doesn't apply to traditional fungible tokens (such as bitcoin and ether). This is why it's important to consider both types of tokens when you're looking at an NFT: non-fungible tokens and fungible tokens.

What is the supply for NFTs?

There are several things to keep in mind when considering the supply of NFTs. The most important thing to keep in mind is that it is all based on trust. NFTs can be used to represent anything, including physical objects. For example, an individual could create a digital token that represents a share of their house. This token could then be used as collateral for a loan or as proof of ownership for their house.

When an individual wants to create a NFT, they need to be aware of how it will affect the supply of the item being represented by the token. For example, if you create a digital token that represents 1/100th of your house, there are now 99 tokens representing 1/100th of your house in circulation (instead of 100). This makes it more difficult for you to sell your entire share because there are now 99 tokens available representing 1/100th of your house (rather than just one).

Another way to think about this is through scarcity. If there are only 100 tokens representing 1/100th of your house, each token has a higher chance at receiving some value because there are fewer tokens available and they are more scarce. It's much easier for people to sell their tokens to other people because they are not competing with other individuals who have a similar share of your house.

Does NFTs have a fixed supply like BTC?

NFTs can have a fixed supply, a limited supply, or an unlimited supply. A token that has a fixed supply is similar to a cryptocurrency with a fixed supply. In the case of NFTs, each NFT is assigned a unique identifier (ERC-721) and can be tracked as it moves from one owner to another.

In the case of CryptoKitties, each CryptoKitty is uniquely identified by its own 256-bit genome that consists of these genes:

Attribute: This gene defines the cat's appearance and gives it its special abilities.

This gene defines the cat's appearance and gives it its special abilities. Genotype: This gene determines the cat's genotype. It consists of 256 bits that determine the DNA sequence for this specific CryptoKitty.

Cutype: This gene contains information about how many times this specific CryptoKitty has been bred or sired by other cats in the network. For example, if a CryptoKitty has a "1" in this gene, it means that it has sired or been sired once.

Cowner: This gene identifies the owner of the CryptoKitty. The owner can be the person who bought the CryptoKitty, a third party, or the CryptoKitty itself.

The owners of a CryptoKitty can also be changed through the use of a smart contract. In this case, the CryptoKitty's owner is simply the person who owns the private key to the Ethereum address that contains this particular CryptoKitty. This makes it possible for third parties to own CryptoKitties and use them as part of their business models.

To summarize, each CryptoKitty has a unique 256-bit genome and an owner who can change over time. The current owner is determined by the private key of an Ethereum address that contains this specific CryptoKitty. In order to change ownership, you must first change ownership in a smart contract and then sign off on it with your private key (in case of a multi-signature smart contract). This makes it possible for someone to "purchase" a unique and rare 256-bit genome in order to breed new cats with special abilities (for example, see KittyVerse).

Unlike other cryptocurrencies, there is no limit on how many NFTs can be created. Instead, NFTs are created in two ways: through "creation" or through "breeding."

Creation: NFTs can be created in the same way that cryptocurrencies are created. This is done by the creation of a new smart contract that contains all of the attributes of a new CryptoKitty.

Breeding: In order to create new NFTs, they must first be bred with other NFTs in order to produce offspring with specific and unique characteristics. For example, a KittyVerse developer might want to create a CryptoKitty with special abilities (for example, unique appearance or certain attributes). In order to do this, they would need to breed this CryptoKitty with another CryptoKitty that has similar or complementary attributes (such as appearance).

The breeding process is somewhat similar to traditional genetic engineering techniques where an organism's DNA is manipulated in order to produce offspring with certain characteristics. However, instead of using genes from existing organisms, you use blockchain-based smart contracts as your DNA blueprint. The process of breeding NFTs is called "breeding" and the act of breeding NFTs is called "siring."

To summarize, NFTs can be created in two ways: through "creation" or through "breeding." In the case of creation, a new smart contract is created that contains all of the attributes of a new CryptoKitty. In the case of breeding, you use blockchain-based smart contracts as your DNA blueprint to produce offspring with specific and unique characteristics.

How do NFTs get their value?

One of the key differences between cryptocurrencies and NFTs is that the supply of a cryptocurrency is fixed. The supply of an NFT can change depending on the creator's intention. This means that if you want to make an NFT, you need to be aware of how it will affect the supply and demand for your token.

The economics behind supply and demand will dictate how much your token is worth. If there are a lot of tokens available, it will be more difficult for people to sell them for a high price because there are many other people trying to sell their tokens as well. On the other hand, if there are fewer tokens available, each individual token will be worth more because it's more scarce and it's easier for people to sell their tokens at a higher price because they aren't competing with as many other individuals.

This concept is most important when thinking about digital collectibles (like CryptoKitties). When CryptoKitties were first released, there were very few kitties in circulation. Each kitty was worth a lot of money because there were very few kitties available.

Now that there are thousands of CryptoKitties in circulation, the price of each kitty has decreased because it's much easier for people to sell their kitties at a high price because there are many other people trying to sell their kitties as well. The same concept applies to any NFT.

If you want your token to be worth a lot of money, you should try and make it scarce so that there are fewer tokens available in circulation.

What takes place in a NFT transaction

1. The producer, or token issuer, is responsible for setting the rules of a game or experience and defining what happens when a user performs an action. The producer can also set the price that users pay to play.

2. The player/user buys access to the game with a non-fungible token (NFT). They may use ETH or other NFTs as well.

3. The player/user interacts with the game using their NFT, which triggers actions and/or events on the blockchain, like transferring ownership of a virtual asset or being awarded a prize. If they win something valuable, they can sell it on an exchange for ETH or other NFTs.
4. Other players may want to buy access to the same game with their own NFTs, but they can't unless they buy one from someone who already owns it. In order to acquire a NFT, you must trade another one for it or purchase it directly from the issuer (the developer). If you choose to trade your NFT for another one on an exchange, you'll be subject to market forces just like any other tradable asset—including volatility and transaction fees!

5. This loop continues until the game or experience ends.

Chapter 5: The Benefits of NFTs

Given the hype surrounding NFTs, it's worth asking whether there are any benefits of NFTs over other blockchain-based asset types. There are a few advantages of NFTs over other assets.

Here are the top benefits and characteristics of NFTs:

1. Ownership

The most obvious benefit of NFTs is that they represent a clear and defined owner. This means that, unlike many other crypto assets, the NFT owner has full control over their asset. This is possible because the NFT is unique and can't be copied or double spent. There are no issues with "theft" of an asset. This is one of the properties of it's non-fungibility.

In addition, NFTs are non-divisible. This means that the owner of an NFT can't choose to "break up" their asset into smaller pieces. If you own a painting, for example, you own the entire painting. You can't sell or trade one inch of it.

NFTs are also indivisible because they represent a digital file or record. It is impossible to physically divide an NFT into two pieces. You can, however, copy an NFT in digital form and then trade or sell the copy instead of the original asset.

The ownership and non-fungibility of NFTs means that owners have full control over their assets and no one else can claim ownership over it. This provides a clear level of security for both developers and users when using NFTs in their applications and games.

For example, if you own a rare asset in a game or application, you know that it is safe and no one else can claim ownership over it. This means that there is no risk of losing your rare asset because it is non-fungible.

2. Transferability

Another benefit of NFTs is that they are very easy to transfer from one person to another. This is possible because the blockchain makes it easy to track transfers of NFTs.

In addition, NFTs are easier to transfer than many other blockchain-based assets because they can be represented by a unique ID number. This ID number can be used by the owner of an asset to quickly and easily trade or sell their asset without having to provide much additional information.

This makes it easy for people to trade or sell their assets, and makes it easier for users of applications and games that use NFTs. For example, a game developer might allow players to quickly sell or trade their rare items with other players using a blockchain-based auction system built into the game. This could be done with a simple transaction ID rather than providing much more information about the asset, like its location in the game or its level of rarity.

Another example is a digital art gallery that allows people to trade or sell their digital artworks quickly and easily. A blockchain-based system could be used to track the ownership of a digital artwork, and allow users to quickly trade or sell their assets using a simple ID number.

3. Authenticity

The authenticity of NFTs is also a key benefit. This is because the blockchain makes it easy to prove that an asset is authentic.

For example, if you are using a game or application that uses NFTs, you can be sure that the assets you have are genuine and not counterfeit. You can easily check this using a blockchain explorer like Etherscan.io or by checking a digital signature or fingerprint of the asset in the game or application.

This means that developers can quickly and easily prove that their assets are authentic and have not been copied or modified in any way. This provides users with confidence when they buy, trade, or sell NFTs within applications and games.

In addition, the authenticity of NFTs makes it easy for developers to keep track of the number of times an asset has been used. This means that they can easily determine how many times an asset has been used, and how many times it has been traded or sold.

This can be done by checking the number of transfers on a blockchain explorer. This makes it easy for developers to understand how popular their assets are, and how much value they might have in the market.

4. Security

The security of NFTs is also one of their key benefits. Because they are represented by a unique ID number, there is no way for someone to "copy" or "clone" an NFT. This means that you can always be sure that your assets are secure and safe from being copied or stolen by someone else.

This is particularly important when using NFTs in applications and games where rare items are used as a form of reward or achievement system for players. For example, if you are using a game that uses NFTs as rewards for players who complete certain levels, you can be sure that those rewards aren't counterfeit because they can't be copied or faked in any way.

5. Customization

The customization of NFTs is also a key benefit. This is because NFTs can be easily customized by developers and users to represent anything they want.

For example, a game developer might create a new type of virtual sword in their game that can be used by players to attack enemies. They could then customize the sword using a set of features that represent the properties of the sword, like its size, length, weight, and number of attack points. This would make it possible for players to collect unique swords with different features and stats that would give them an advantage over other players in the game.

The customization of NFTs also makes it possible for developers to create "generic" assets that can be customized by users. For example, an application developer might create a virtual sword asset that has no special features or stats on it at all. Instead, they could allow users to customize the weapon by adding additional features and stats themselves using an in-game editor or system built into the application itself. This would allow users to create custom swords with special stats and features based on their own preferences and requirements in the game or application itself.

The ability to customize NFTs makes it possible for developers to create assets that are unique and represent whatever they want. This can be done by simply changing the features and stats of an asset, or even the image of the asset itself.

6. Permissionless

The permissionless nature of NFTs is also a key benefit. This is because NFTs can be used by anyone, without needing permission from anyone else.

This means that developers can quickly and easily create new assets and tokens for their applications and games without having to get approval from anyone else first. This provides a level of freedom for developers that isn't possible with other blockchain-based assets like tokens or coins. It also means that they don't have to worry about any restrictions on the types of assets they create or how many they make available in their applications or games.

In addition, the permissionless nature of NFTs makes it easy for users to trade or sell their assets on open marketplaces without having to get approval from anyone else first. This makes it possible for users to quickly and easily trade or sell their assets, and provides a way for them to do so in a safe and secure way.

The permissionless nature of NFTs is also beneficial for developers because it makes it easy for them to use their own assets within their applications or games. This is because they don't have to worry about restrictions on the types of assets they can use, or how many they can make available.

7. Decentralization

This is a really cool topic. It's the idea that blockchains allow people to create their own assets. With this technology, you can create a token that represents a specific item or piece of property. It's essentially a digital asset that can be owned and transferred. This means that there is no need for a middleman like an auction house or real estate agent.

Blockchain technology allows you to cut out the middleman and keep all of the profits for yourself. It also means that you have complete control over your items and property, as opposed to having to trust a third party with it. You have complete control over your items, whether it's something like real estate or digital art.

As NFTs rely on the blockchain, they are always decentralised. This means that you don't have to trust a third party to manage your assets. The blockchain is completely transparent and you can see everything that is happening with your digital asset. This means that there is no chance of the item being taken away from you or altered in any way.

8. Transparency

Transparency is an important part of the blockchain technology behind NFTs. Every transaction made on the blockchain is publicly available for everyone to see. This allows for complete transparency and there is no chance of anyone altering your data without being caught.

9. Easy Trading

NFTs allow for easy trading between users. They can be traded as many times as you want and are often easier to sell than physical items like paintings or cars. You simply create a digital token representing the item, then put it up for sale on an exchange where people can buy it using cryptocurrencies like Bitcoin or Ethereum (there are also exchanges for NFTs themselves). The token represents the item in question and if you decide to sell it, all that needs to happen is the token being transferred from one user to another. The item itself doesn't need to be transferred because it already exists on the blockchain.

Chapter 6: Are NFTs Really Revolutionary?

In many ways, NFTs have the potential to be revolutionary. They are an asset class that has previously been nonexistent, and they have already shown themselves to be a major disruptor in the world of gaming.

However, NFTs are not perfect. There are many challenges that developers will need to overcome if they want to make NFTs a reality for everyone. This is where things get tricky.

NFTs, by their very nature, cannot function without some form of blockchain technology or another similar technology. This presents a major problem for most developers because the current blockchain space is relatively inaccessible for developers who don't have the right technical knowledge or resources at their disposal. For this reason, there is a strong need for better developer tools and more robust blockchain infrastructure if NFTs are going to achieve mainstream adoption anytime soon.

In addition to these challenges, it will take some time before players get used to having digital assets that can be traded freely on secondary markets and even longer before people start spending money on digital assets instead of spending money on traditional video games themselves. That being said, as long as there is progress made on both of these fronts (developer tools and more robust infrastructure), then it won't be long before NFTs become a reality for everyone.

NFTs are still in their infancy, but there is no denying that they have the potential to be revolutionary. They have already shown themselves to be major disruptors in the world of gaming, and if developers continue to push forward with them, then it won't be long before they are used by the mainstream population.

However, there are still many challenges that developers will need to overcome if they want to make NFTs a reality for everyone.

What makes NFTs so special:

NFTs are a special type of digital asset that has never existed before. These assets are very similar to traditional digital assets, but they have the potential to be far more valuable and interesting than traditional digital assets.

Traditional digital assets have existed for many years now, but they haven't really changed much over the years. With NFTs, however, there is a possibility that they will change a lot in the coming years. They can change by becoming more secure, by getting more adoption from developers and gamers alike, and by getting more widespread support from exchanges and other organizations.

Because of this, NFTs could become far more valuable than traditional digital assets. This is because of their potential to create true ownership over in-game items and even other things such as land or even tangible goods such as cars or houses in the future.

Another reason why NFTs are so special is because they are truly open source for anyone who wants to use them in their games or on their platforms. Because of this, developers can create unique games and applications without worrying about copyright infringement or other legal issues that may arise when using NFTs with other technologies like blockchain technology or smart contracts. This is because everything is already built into the NFT protocol, and everything is open source.

However, there are still some challenges that developers will need to overcome if they want to make NFTs a reality for everyone. These challenges include the fact that NFTs can only function with blockchain technology or another similar technology. This means that most developers don't have the right technical knowledge or resources at their disposal in order to create NFTs for their games. This is why there is a strong need for better developer tools and more robust blockchain infrastructure if NFTs are going to achieve mainstream adoption anytime soon.

What are the conditions for NFTs to go mainstream?

It's an excellent question, but one that is difficult to answer. Theoretically, NFTs could be used in a variety of applications and even have their own currency that can be used to buy/sell items or pay for services.

However, the actual execution of this is not so simple. NFTs need to solve two main problems: scalability and interoperability. Let's explore each of these in more detail.

Scalability

The NFT ecosystem has two problems that prevent it from being truly scalable: blockchain bloat and slow transactions.

To understand blockchain bloat, we must first understand the difference between State Channels and Off-Chain Transactions (OCT). A State Channel is a communication channel between parties in which transactions are conducted off-chain instead of on-chain (which is what most blockchains do). This means that transactions do not need to be broadcasted across the entire network but only between the parties involved in the transaction itself. This saves time and computational power as well as reducing blockchain bloat by limiting transactions to just those relevant to a specific contract or smart contract operation (in our case, an NFT transaction). To learn more about State Channels, click here.

OCT refers to the fact that transactions can be conducted off-chain (in a State Channel) or on-chain. For example, Ethereum currently uses on-chain transactions, meaning that every transaction has to be processed by the entire network.

NFTs have their own unique scalability issues due to the nature of NFTs themselves. The Ethereum blockchain is currently incapable of processing all of the on-chain transactions needed for an NFT ecosystem (e.g., all transactions related to auctions, transactions, and transfers). This is because it takes an extremely long time for Ethereum's Proof of Work (PoW) algorithm to process a transaction. And even then, it's not guaranteed that your transaction will be included in the next block (it could take hours or even days). This means that users are limited in how much they can transact within a certain time period — if you try to transact too much at once, your transaction may never go through. It's just not scalable enough for mass adoption yet.

The solution? State Channels! By using State Channels we can eliminate some of these issues by allowing users to conduct NFT transactions off-chain, and by limiting the number of transactions to only those relevant to the contract or smart contract operation. This allows for faster and more efficient transactions that don't have to be processed by the entire network.
But how can we do this with NFTs? Currently, State Channels are not compatible with NFTs. This is because an NFT transaction is essentially a simple "message" between two parties, meaning that it doesn't contain any important information about the transaction itself (e.g., "the sender transferred X amount of tokens to the receiver at address Y"). So how can we create a State Channel that works with NFTs?

We need a protocol that allows us to use State Channels with an NFT — one which gives us:

Privacy: State Channels allow users to conduct transactions off-chain without broadcasting them on-chain. This means that they are not visible to other users on the blockchain (or other blockchains). But in order for this to work, all parties involved in a transaction must be able to see the details of the transaction. So how can we ensure privacy while using State Channels?

Fungibility: As mentioned above, a major issue with NFTs is that each token has a unique identifier, meaning that each token is not interchangeable. This means that if I were to send you a token

54

with an identifier that you don't recognize, you would reject it. This is because it is essentially useless to you — there's no way for you to determine whether or not the token was sent to me by mistake or if I am trying to scam you by sending you an unusable token. But what if we could eliminate this problem?

Uniqueness: State Channels only allow us to broadcast transactions on-chain in the case of an error or dispute (i.e., a dispute arises when the two parties involved in the transaction disagree on what happened). So how can we prevent this from happening?

State Channels are a great solution for scalability issues, but they cannot be used for NFTs without these three requirements above. So how can we solve these problems? Well, let's take a look at some solutions and their limitations:

Solution 1: NFTs Without State Channels (on-chain)

This option does not require any protocol changes. It simply requires that users use the Ethereum blockchain directly to conduct NFT transactions. In this case, all transactions are visible to everyone on the blockchain. This means that there is no privacy or fungibility issue, but it also means that the network would have to process a lot of on-chain transactions (e.g., every transaction between every NFT owner).

This would put a huge strain on the Ethereum network, and scalability issues would be even worse than they are now. This is because every transaction has to be processed by every node in the network — it's not possible for transactions to be processed by only two parties (as in State Channels).

Solution 2: Non-fungible Tokens (NFTs) With State Channels (off-chain)

This option requires protocol changes that allow for privacy and fungibility of NFTs while using State Channels. This solution is theoretically possible but difficult to implement. It would require some type of anonymization layer for each token so that two tokens with different identifiers can be used interchangeably within a single transaction (i.e., it allows you to send me an NFT even if I don't recognize its identifier). This can only be done if all NFTs are stored in a single address, meaning that all tokens are fungible and there is no privacy issue.

The problem with this solution is that it requires each NFT to be stored in a single address, meaning that they are not truly non-fungible. For example, let's say that you created a CryptoKitty and you want to sell it for some ETH. If all NFTs are stored in a single address, then anyone can easily see the value of your CryptoKitty and buy it from you (or just copy your CryptoKitty's identifier and make their own copy). This means that you would lose ownership of your CryptoKitty without getting paid.

In order for this solution to work, we need to come up with some way to hide the value of each token while still allowing for privacy (so that no one can see which tokens are owned by which users). The best way to do this would be through Ring Signatures — an advanced cryptographic method used for ring signatures (and often used in cryptocurrencies) that allows users to conceal their identities while sending transactions. But even then, there is still a risk of loss because if someone were able to copy your NFT's identifier, they could still copy your token. This is because Ring Signatures only allow you to conceal the transaction sender's identity, not the sender's address.

Solution 3: Non-fungible Tokens (NFTs) With State Channels (off-chain) and Protocol Changes

This option requires protocol changes that allow for privacy and fungibility of NFTs while using State Channels. The protocol changes required for this solution are similar to those required for Solution 2 above, but with one major difference: they require that all NFTs be stored in a single address — meaning that all tokens are fungible and there is no privacy issue.

But what if we could eliminate the possibility of copying an NFT's identifier? Well, we can! But first we need to understand how Ethereum works with smart contracts. Currently, all smart contracts in Ethereum are stored on the blockchain. This means that any information contained within a smart contract is visible to everyone on the blockchain (i.e., all smart contracts are public). So how can we solve this problem? We need to store only an encrypted version of our smart contract on the blockchain instead of the entire contract.

So how can we do this? We need to create a way to encrypt smart contracts on-chain using a blockchain-specific encryption method. There are a few different ways to do this, but we'll use Shamir's Secret Sharing (SSS) for our example. SSS allows us to split up a secret into multiple parts and store them in different locations — it's like putting all of your money in different banks so that you can't lose it all if one bank fails.

So let's say that you want to sell your CryptoKitty for some ETH, but you don't want anyone else to be able to copy your CryptoKitty. You could split up your CryptoKitty smart contract into two parts:

The first part contains information about the buyer (e.g., their Ethereum address) and the amount of ETH they will receive after the transaction has been completed (e.g., 2 ETH). The second part contains information about the seller (e.g., their Ethereum address) and the unique identifier of your CryptoKitty.

When these two parts are put together, they form an encrypted version of your CryptoKitty smart contract.

So now, instead of the entire CryptoKitty smart contract being stored on the blockchain, only an encrypted version of it is stored on the blockchain. And you can do this for every CryptoKitty you own!

The downside to this solution is that the NFTs must be stored in a single address — meaning that all NFTs are fungible and there is no privacy issue. This is why we need protocol changes for this solution to work. If we were able to store each NFT in its own address, then we wouldn't need protocol changes. But since we can't do that right now, we need protocol changes. The good news is that the new "Ethereum 2.0" update for Ethereum will likely have all of these necessary protocol changes built-in by default — so if you want to build a state channel-based NFT platform, you should use Ethereum 2.0.

Chapter 7: The NFT Boom

As we have covered in the previous chapters, NFTs are digital assets that are non-fungible, transferable, and tradable. They can represent almost anything from physical assets to in-game items to even celebrities.

It is the last category that has been the focus of much of the recent excitement around NFTs. The advent of blockchain technology has allowed for the creation of digital assets which can be transferred peer-to-peer and therefore do not require a centralized third party such as a company or government to verify their authenticity.

As we have covered in previous chapters, this has had massive implications for businesses and governments who are looking to streamline their operations and save on overhead costs. However, what about the average person?

The recent explosion of blockchain-based collectibles, particularly on the Ethereum blockchain, has created a new class of asset that can be owned by anyone in the world and which has been dubbed Crypto Collectibles.

While this sounds exciting to many people, there is still a lot of confusion about what exactly a crypto collectible is and how it differs from other crypto assets such as cryptocurrencies.

Is there a market bubble for NFTs?

Going back to the basics of a bubble, there is clearly an extreme spike in the value of non-fungible tokens. But, how long will this bubble last? This is a question that only time can answer. It is possible that NFTs are in a bubble and that the bubble will pop, but we won't know for sure until the market adjusts to a new price.

I am not trying to be a doomsayer, but there are a few factors that could indicate that the NFT market is in a bubble. The crypto market is known for its volatility and there are times when things seem to spiral out of control. We've seen the crypto market experience some of these bubbles, and while they are painful for some, it is important to remember that many of these markets have recovered. It is possible that the NFT market will recover as well.

What is driving the current rise in NFTs?

1. Speculation

The crypto market is full of speculators and people who believe that they can predict the future. These people have been buying NFTs in hopes that the value will continue to rise. This type of behavior isn't necessarily a bad thing, but it can create a bit of volatility. When the market fluctuates, some people get hurt and others make money. The goal is to make money, but many people aren't able to predict how high or low the price will go.

2. Media Attention

Many of the top NFTs are being used in games and virtual worlds. There are some crypto art projects that are making it big in the media and social circles. When something gets this much attention, it is easy for speculators to jump on board and buy NFTs at a higher price. When there is more demand for NFTs, the price will increase.

3. Limited Supply

There are a limited number of NFTs that are being created each year for each project. The amount of tokens that are available at any given time is being reduced because of the projects that are creating new tokens. Some people believe that this reduction in supply will lead to a higher price, but it isn't necessarily true. A higher price will only occur if there is more demand for the tokens.

4. The rise in popularity of decentralized games and virtual worlds

The popularity of decentralized games and virtual worlds is on the rise. There are many projects that are creating new games and virtual worlds that will utilize NFTs. Some of these projects have been successful, while others have failed. When a project fails, it could mean that the value of the NFTs associated with that project will decrease.

The Future of NFTs

The future of non-fungible tokens is uncertain. The current value is not sustainable and the market is overpriced, but this doesn't mean that there won't be a recovery. There are a lot of people who believe in the future of NFTs and crypto art, so there could be a rebound in the near future. We can only wait and see what happens to the market in the next few months or years.

Let's take a look at the popular NFT collectible categories.

Crypto Art

The most popular category of crypto collectibles is art. As we have covered in previous chapters, the earliest blockchain-based digital assets were essentially digital files such as music or videos. However, one problem with this was that it could be easily copied and shared without any centralized entity to verify its authenticity.

A solution to this problem came in the form of Crypto Art. By putting a piece of art on the blockchain, you can now ensure that only one copy exists and no one can copy it without breaking the encryption. This means that artists can now sell digital versions of their artwork and guarantee that no one else will be able to print out copies of it or sell them for profit.

The result has been a number of companies that have popped up selling digital versions of artwork for various prices. However, they are not alone in this market. Many other types of companies have begun to sell NFTs which represent physical items such as cars or clothing and they even go so far as to sell digital assets which represent real-world assets such as a home or business building!

However, while this seems exciting, there are some limitations to what you can do with these NFTs. For example, you cannot actually transfer ownership of the underlying asset that the NFT represents. This means that you cannot sell the car or home you own, but you can sell your NFT of it.

This is also true for crypto art as well. While you can technically buy a digital version of an artwork, you cannot actually purchase the physical artwork itself. In order to do this, you would have to purchase the actual physical piece of art and then simply verify its authenticity using a blockchain-based platform such as Ascribe or Proof of Existence.

The result is that many companies have created NFTs which represent assets which they don't actually own and are therefore just digital representations of those assets. This can be very confusing for people who are not familiar with blockchain technology and it may be difficult for them to distinguish between companies that are actually selling physical assets versus companies that are selling digital representations of those assets.

Let's take a look at some examples of different types of crypto art:

Crypto Collectibles:

While Crypto Art is popular among blockchain enthusiasts, most people who aren't involved in cryptocurrency probably haven't heard about it yet. The result is that many crypto collectible enthusiasts have decided to take their hobby a step further and create blockchain-based digital assets that represent real-world items.

In order to do this, you need to know how to code smart contracts on the Ethereum blockchain. The result is that there are a number of companies which have sprung up which offer services for creating crypto collectibles such as CryptoKitties and Etheremon.

The main difference between these NFTs and crypto art is that with these collectibles, you can actually transfer ownership of the underlying asset that the NFT represents. This means that you can buy a CryptoKitty from someone else and then transfer ownership of it to someone else who will pay you money for it. You can also sell an Etheremon or any other crypto collectible on an exchange such as OpenSea or RareBits in exchange for cryptocurrency.

As we have covered in previous chapters, this is one of the most exciting aspects of blockchain technology because it allows us to create new types of assets which we could not have done before. However, there are still some limitations with these assets as well:

There are no laws in place yet regarding the use of NFTs or crypto collectibles in general so there may be some risks associated with purchasing them.

There is still a lot of confusion regarding the legality of these assets. Many countries have not yet created laws that allow for the use of crypto collectibles or NFTs and there are no laws in place which would protect you if someone sold you a crypto collectible which was fake or even if it were stolen from someone else.

There is also a lack of information regarding these assets and how they work. As we have covered in previous chapters, there are still many people who do not understand how blockchain technology works and how it differs from traditional fiat currency. This can make it difficult for them to understand what they are buying when they purchase a crypto collectible or NFT.

The result is that many people who are interested in buying crypto collectibles and NFTs are not yet sure what to buy or where to buy them from so there has been very little innovation in this area compared to other types of crypto assets such as cryptocurrencies.

However, this does not mean that the future for these types of assets is bleak. There is still much potential for these assets as we will see below:

Virtual Reality:

As we have covered in previous chapters, one major drawback with NFTs is that they are not very tangible. If you own a CryptoKitty, you can see it on your computer screen and it can look cute, but you cannot hold it in your hand or put it on a shelf.

This has led to the creation of another category of crypto collectibles which aims to address this problem. These are called Virtual Reality Assets and they aim to create digital assets which represent physical objects such as a statue or even a person. The result is that users can view these virtual assets in 3D VR worlds and have them appear as though they are actually there.

While this seems like an exciting innovation, there are still some limitations with these assets:

The graphics technology for virtual reality is still not very advanced so most of these assets do not look very realistic or life-like. This means that most people would not be willing to pay high prices for them because they would simply be unable to tell the difference between the digital asset and the real-world item it represents.

It is also very difficult to verify the authenticity of these virtual reality assets since there is no centralized entity responsible for doing so. The result is that someone could easily take a photo of an object from the internet and use it as the basis for a virtual reality asset. This means that there is no way to verify whether the virtual reality asset is real or not.

There are also very few places where you can buy or sell these assets so it can be difficult to find someone who is willing to trade them with you.

In order to address these issues, we will need more advanced graphics technology and a larger user base for these virtual reality assets in order for them to be truly viable.

Games

The second category of crypto collectibles are games. The first major collectible game was CryptoKitties, which is a game where players can collect and breed digital cats.

These cats are each unique and therefore cannot be copied or replicated, which is the fundamental property of NFTs. Players can trade these cats, and their breeding history, on the marketplace.
The game was a huge success, with more than $23 million worth of transactions in the first two months alone. It is estimated that over 3 million crypto kitties have been sold to date.

This is a massive amount of activity for a game that was not even originally intended to be played as a collectible game. However, after CryptoKitties became popular with crypto traders, the developers decided to launch CryptoKitties as a full-fledged collectible game rather than just an experiment in non-fungible tokens.
This shows that the world of NFTs and blockchain games is very much still in its infancy and will continue to evolve as developers figure out how best to implement NFTs into their games. This evolution will likely result in games that are more focused on gameplay rather than just being collectibles or blockchain-based assets.

Another exciting trend is the recent release of new games based on popular IPs such as Pokemon Go and Harry Potter, which are based on NFTs owned by a company called Enjin. In this case, there are no actual digital assets or digital creatures created for the game, but the game is a gateway to interact with the digital assets that players already own.

The first game to be released by Enjin is War of Crypto, which is a game where players can use their existing digital assets to battle each other. This means that all players have access to their digital collectibles regardless of whether they have downloaded the game or not.

War of Crypto is also an interesting case because it combines both blockchain and non-blockchain elements into one game. The collectible items in the game are non-fungible tokens, while all the gameplay elements are stored on the Ethereum blockchain. This means that all items in the game can be traded freely and without having to worry about cheating or unfair gameplay mechanics.

This combination of NFTs and blockchain technology has resulted in a revolutionary gaming experience that offers true ownership of digital assets as well as trustless gameplay which ensures fairness for all participants.

It will be exciting to see how this trend develops as more companies begin creating games based on NFTs they already own, rather than having to create new ones from scratch. This will likely result in more interesting gameplay mechanics as well as more NFT games being created over time. As such, it is very likely that this trend will continue to grow over the next few years.

Brands

The third category of crypto collectibles is brands. As we have seen in previous chapters, NFTs can represent a wide variety of assets from companies to celebrities to digital pets. However, this can be difficult as not all assets are transferable and some require a centralized authority to verify their authenticity.

Brands are an example of how this has been done correctly. By having an authoritative third party verify the authenticity of each brand asset, brands can create a secure environment for trading their assets on the blockchain and also set certain parameters for how they can be used by other parties.

One of the first major brands to do this was in the music industry with Ujo Music. This platform allows artists to sell their music directly to fans and users by issuing each track as an NFT token which then represents ownership of that track on the blockchain. This has several benefits over other forms of content distribution such as Spotify and iTunes:

Fans pay directly for the content, so artists don't have to pay large fees to middlemen like Apple or Spotify. Artists receive 100% of their earnings from every sale instead of being subject to profit-sharing agreements with distributors like Apple or Spotify which take a large cut off the top. Fans get access to behind-the-scenes content like videos and interviews.

This model is a great example of how brands can leverage the power of blockchain technology to create better experiences for their customers.
In addition, brands can also use their NFTs to create a variety of branded assets which users can then purchase with their tokens. For example, an artist might create a collectible figurine which is based on the image of one of their album covers. This figurine could then be purchased with Ujo Music tokens and would then represent ownership of that album on the blockchain.

This model allows artists to reach a wider audience and creates an incentive for people to buy their music while still earning money for themselves.

The bottom line is that brands have been slow to adopt blockchain technology due to its decentralized nature, but once they realize the benefits it can bring them, we will see a lot more companies adopting this model in the future.

Famous People

Another category of crypto collectibles are those based on famous people such as celebrities or sports stars. The first company to do this was CryptoKitties, which created digital kittens based on real-world celebrities such as Paris Hilton and Grumpy Cat. Each kitten represented ownership of that celebrity's digital avatar and users could trade them just like any other collectible token. This led to several bizarre instances where someone would purchase a cat token from another user and then immediately sell it back to the original owner.

Since then, several other projects have emerged which are creating collectibles based on celebrities such as these coins from Crypto Celebrities.

As with any crypto asset, these collectibles are tradable and can be transferred to other users. This has led to a growing trend of celebrity endorsements of blockchain projects and even in-game gambling using celebrities' avatars. For example, Crypto Celebrities created a game called "Crypto Space Commander" where users could play as their favorite celebrity avatar in a spaceship simulator. They also created a casino style game where users could gamble their token against other players for fun or even for real money. This all happened without the celebrity needing to get involved or even knowing about it, which made it a huge success.

Music

Music is the perfect example of an asset that can be represented by a NFT. In this case, the music file itself is represented by a token which can be stored on a blockchain. This is similar to how you can download MP3s from iTunes or listen to Spotify.

What makes these assets different from their physical counterparts is that they are decentralized and therefore censorship-resistant. You can store them in your own wallet and send them to other people who have the token's public address, meaning you don't need to go through any central entity such as Apple or Spotify.

You could theoretically send the same music file over and over again without paying any additional fees, as opposed to streaming services where you have to pay every time you listen to your favorite song. You also do not need to pay for storage as it is stored on the blockchain network itself, so there are no extra costs associated with it other than buying the token in the first place.

The biggest issue with these types of tokens is that there aren't many of them out there yet, but this will likely change in the near future as more people realize how useful they are for storing digital assets such as music files.

In order for a music file to be an NFT, it must be unique and therefore impossible to replicate. The file itself cannot be duplicated as it would make the token useless. This means that the music file itself must be one-of-a-kind and the owner of the token must have a verified copy of it.

In this case, the token itself is stored on a blockchain network and can be transferred peer-to-peer without any intermediaries. This means that if you have a particular song on your computer, you can send it to someone else in its entirety with no fees associated with it other than the initial cost of buying the token in the first place.
You do not need to download or listen to it from a centralized third party such as Apple or Spotify. The token acts as proof of ownership and can then be stored on your computer for future use or transferred to another person via blockchain transactions.

Chapter 8: Future Potential of NFTs

The idea of a digital asset which has ownership, which can be exchanged and traded, is not new. Crypto-collectibles are essentially digital assets that are designed to be unique, and only one instance of each token can exist. This has created a marketplace for collectibles where users can purchase and trade these tokens.

The future of crypto-collectibles is very bright, with more and more users entering the market. Although there are some key challenges that need to be overcome before they can be considered mainstream.

In this chapter, we will discuss the future potential of NFTs and how it will change the world.

Physical Goods Utility:

Physical goods utility is the idea that you can use an item to derive value from it. This is why many physical goods have a resale value.

For example, if you own a digital asset of your house, you can potentially use it as collateral for a loan. As long as the physical asset exists, the digital asset has value.

It's important to note that there are not any digital assets that currently offer this utility, however this is one of the main reasons why crypto-collectibles have gained so much popularity.

In this section we will explore some of the key benefits of owning NFTs and how they can be used in the future:

Non-Fungible Crypto-Collectibles are Proof of Ownership:

Crypto-collectibles are designed to be unique tokens which mean that they cannot be duplicated or forged. This creates a very unique digital asset which can be used as proof of ownership for certain physical goods. For example, if you own a CryptoKitty that is modeled after your pet cat, then there will only ever be one instance of this token in existence. You could use this token as proof of ownership for your pet cat, however there is no reason why you could not use it as proof of ownership for other physical goods.

In the future, we could see this type of utility being used for art, gold, real estate and many other physical goods. The idea that you can store your ownership of a physical good on the blockchain is a very exciting concept.

Think of it as digital inheritance. When you die, your digital assets are transferred to the rightful owners, and it's also a way to prove that you are the owner of an item.

Protecting Digital Written Content:

The problem with written content on the internet is that it can be copied and shared with ease. However, with a NFT, this becomes a lot more difficult.

If you own a digital asset that represents your written content, then you can use it as proof of ownership. For example, if you own the digital asset of a blog post or article that you have written, then you can prove that it is yours and there is only one instance of it in existence.

The same principle applies to artwork and music. As long as the token represents ownership of the artwork or music file, then there will only ever be one instance of this token in existence.

Artwork or Music:

In order for artwork to be truly unique, the artist must design it specifically for the piece of art itself. This means that every single aspect must be designed by the artist themselves which means they will have complete control over how many instances exist on the blockchain. They will also have complete control over how they are used in the future (such as selling them on a marketplace). As long as an artist has designed their artwork for a specific piece of art and each piece is uniquely designed for each other, then there will only ever be one instance in existence on the blockchain. This means that you can prove ownership of the artwork without the risk of someone copying it.

The same principle applies to music. If an artist creates a specific piece of music and records it, then they can also prove ownership over that specific piece of music. The key difference between art and music is that in order for a piece of art to be unique, the artist must design it specifically for that piece of art. Whereas with music, it's more about recording the specific sound at a specific time in history. This means that if you own a token which represents your digital content, then you can use it as proof of ownership for any physical goods which derive value from this content.

Trading NFTs:

Crypto-collectibles are not only designed to be unique tokens which represent ownership, but they are also designed to be collectible items. This means that people will collect them because they want to own a large number of them and build up their collection. For example, people will buy CryptoKitties in order to build up their collection and add value to their collection by breeding them with other CryptoKitties or trading them on an exchange for ETH or other cryptocurrencies.

This is why many people think that crypto-collectibles will become a mainstream market in the future. As more and more users enter the market, it will create a huge demand for these tokens which could lead to an increase in their value.

In the future, we could see a shift away from buying NFTs for their utility value, and instead users will buy them as collectibles. This is similar to the way that people collect trading cards or rare coins. However, there are still many challenges that need to be overcome before this can happen.

Tackling the issue of digital counterfeit goods:

NFTs have the potential to create a digital library of sorts. You can store your music, art, books and collectibles in a digital library where no one can counterfeit them. As long as you own the digital asset, no one can take it away from you. This is one of the many ways in which NFTs are trying to address the issue of counterfeit goods.

For example, let's say you own a rare copy of Game of Thrones and want to sell it to someone. With the help of NFTs, you can store all the details about your digital asset in a secure blockchain and sell it to someone else.

In addition, you can also verify the authenticity of your digital asset by storing it in a digital library where other people can see that you are the owner of that particular digital asset. This is something which cannot be done with physical goods.

Tackling the issue of data ownership:

Another potential use case for NFTs is tackling the issue of data ownership. Right now, there are many centralized companies which own and store our data like Facebook, Google etc. And they don't give us access to our own data even if we want to get rid of them as our service providers. For example, if I am using Facebook or Google services, I don't have any rights over my personal data that these companies collect from me and use for their own benefit (to target ads). So, they are collecting my personal information like my location history, browsing history etc and selling it to third parties without my consent or knowledge (which is totally illegal).

But, NFTs can help us solve this problem. We can create our own digital assets like a website, blog or any other digital asset and store it in a decentralized platform. Then, we can sell these digital assets to other people. Once the transaction is done, no one can take away your data from you. So, if you are using Facebook or Google services, you don't have to give them access to your personal data (and you don't have to pay them for it). Instead, you can use their services and get paid for it by selling your digital assets to them.

This is the potential of NFTs that we haven't seen yet. As more and more platforms are going to be built on top of Ethereum, we will see more applications of NFTs in the future.

Authenticating Land Ownership:

Land ownership is one of the biggest issues in the world today. You can easily find out if someone owns a land or not by looking at their public records, but it's not easy to prove that you own a land.

For example, let's say you own a land in Canada and want to sell it to someone else. In order to do that, you will have to go through a lot of paperwork and follow a very long process. Not only that, you will also have to pay heavy taxes for selling your land. And after all this, there is no guarantee that the buyer will not steal your land from you later on. This is because most of the time people can forge their documents and make fake IDs.
So, how can NFTs help solve this problem?

NFTs have the potential to create digital identities for land owners which can be verified by anyone using blockchain technology. In addition, we can also store information about our lands in an immutable ledger which cannot be forged or tampered with. So, if you are trying to sell your land in Canada then anyone who is interested in buying it can verify your ownership of that particular piece of land just by checking out the public records.

In addition, you can also prove that you own a land by showing your digital identity to the person who is interested in buying it. And this will be much easier than showing them your physical documents and proving that you own a land.

As more and more platforms are going to be built on top of Ethereum, we will see more applications of NFTs in the future.

Conclusion

NFTs are the future of crypto, and they are already changing the way we see the world. Whether you are interested in gaming, digital art, or digital collectibles, NFTs have something for everyone. This new technology is paving the way for the future of crypto and blockchain, and it will be exciting to see how it develops over time.

As the saying goes, "The future is now."

There are so many potential use cases for NFTs, and so many different types of assets you can create. The possibilities are endless, and the future is looking bright.

The issues that NFTs are able to solve, such as asset management, make them a perfect addition to the crypto world. NFTs have already become one of the most talked about aspects of blockchain technology, and they are sure to have a big impact on the future of crypto.

Remember that NFTs are a type of non-fungible token, and they can be created on any blockchain. It is up to you to decide what kind of asset you want to create, and how you want to use it. You can also sell your NFTs to make a profit, or use them to do something good for the world.

NFTs are here to revolutionize the way we trade and value digital assets. NFTs are already a big part of the crypto world, and they will continue to grow in popularity as time goes on. The future's looking bright for NFTs, and they are sure to have a big impact on the crypto world.

This book has given you a brief overview of NFTs, and what they are capable of. You now know what an NFT is, how they work, and why they are so important.

The future is now, and the future is NFTs.

www.ingramcontent.com/pod-product-compliance
Lightning Source LLC
Chambersburg PA
CBHW070317240526
45467CB00045B/601